BRENDA ROSS'
CRAFT
COLLECTION

Christmas Table Decorations

with
Valerie Janitch

Editor
Brenda Ross

Photography
Melvin Grey

Illustrations
Penny Brown

COLNE PROMOTIONS

First published in 1994 by
Colne Promotions
PO Box 420
Colney Heath
St Albans
Herts AL4 0YA

ISBN 1 899539 02 6

Design and pre-press production by John Boulden, Byfleet

Printed by Crowes, Norwich

Contents

Step by step instructions are given for each project, with references where appropriate to specific techniques explained in the basics section at the back of the book.

...mily nativity	4
...lace cards	10
...has cottage	14
...naypole	22
...wreaths	26
...g choristers	31
	34
...bon roses	34
...terfly bows	35
...ted braid	36
...king a pompon	37
...wing faces and features	38
...ving an egg	39
...king and curling paper	39
...sferring a tracing and ...ng a template	40
...rs and suggested materials	41

...tions in this book you require only basic equipment ...most homes. All measurements are shown in both ...l. Use one or the other, but do not mix them or ...y are worked out independently and whichever you choose you will get a successful result. Where two measurements are stated, such as for a piece of paper, the depth is given first, followed by the width.

The projects in this book are intended for decorations only and are not suitable as toys for young children.

Holy family nativity

This group encapsulates the spirit of Christmas, with Mary and Joseph
gazing at the newborn baby. The soft drapery is all paper, and so are the
figures underneath – even the heads. This simple scene is also very
simple to make.

The figure of Joseph is 18cm (7in) tall, and Mary is 14cm (5½in) tall, The width of the whole family is about 15cm (6in) and they are framed in a balsa wood stable that measures 20cm (8in) high x 22cm (8¾in) wide. Balsa wood can be bought in strips in hobby shops. It is cut with a sharp knife and metal rule, and can be held together with glue and pins so you do not have to be a carpenter to handle it!

Note: Tissue sizes vary slightly, so use your own judgement and adjust the measurements given if necessary.

MATERIALS

Medium-weight white paper – for body foundations and haloes.

Soft-ply paper table napkins or face tissues, in white and light and dark shades of brown and blue – for the clothing – plus white face tissues for padding out the bodies.

Two flesh-tinted turned paper balls, 3.5cm (1⅜in) in diameter – for Joseph's and Mary's heads – and one ball 2cm (¾in) diameter, for Jesus' head.

Seven pipe cleaners 15cm (6in) long – for the 'skeletons' of the figures.

Twilleys stranded embroidery wool – for hair and Joseph's beard: three 76cm (30in) strands in grey for Joseph, four strands in brown for Mary, and one strand in honey for Jesus.

80cm (32in) of 1.5mm (¹⁄₁₆in) wide satin ribbon, or use narrow braid – for Joseph's headband.

60cm (⅝yd) of 1.5mm (¹⁄₁₆in) wide satin ribbon, or use fine cord etc – for Joseph's girdle.

20cm (8in) of gold lurex ribbon, at least 2.5cm (1in) wide – for haloes.

Very narrow gold braid, tiny pearl trimming etc – for edging haloes.

Sepia watercolour pencil, ballpoint pen etc – for features.

Cotton reel and modelling clay or Stick 'n' fix – for Mary to sit on.

White sewing thread – for binding Mary's arms.

Adhesive tape.

Double-sided tape – not essential but useful.

Wallpaper paste – for Mary's hair.

Clear adhesive.

Pieces of balsa wood, 3mm (⅛in) thick, to make the stable – see step 21 to gauge the amount needed.

Brown ink or watercolour etc – for staining the balsa wood.

A little dried foliage – for decoration.

Clear adhesive and short pins.

Joseph

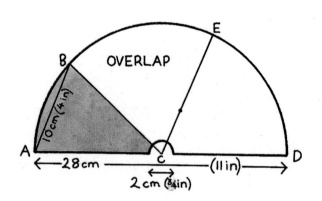

1 *To make the figure of Joseph, draw a 28cm (11in) diameter semi-circle on medium-weight paper, using compasses, with a 2cm (¾in) semi-circle at the centre. Measure point B at the end of a straight line 10cm (4in) from A and rule a line between B and C. Measure and mark the centrepoint between B and D, then rule the line C-E straight through it. Cut out, cutting away the shaded area.*

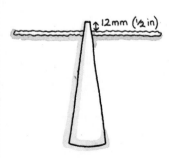

2 *Curve one half round over the other, so that the two straight edges are level with the ruled line, making a cone of double thickness paper. Tape the whole join outside, and at intervals inside. Make two holes, opposite each other, about 12mm (½in) from the top of the cone, and push a pipe cleaner through so that it protrudes equally at each side, forming arms.*

3 Cut a face tissue in half to pad the arms; each piece should be approximately the size given here.
Fold one piece in half lengthways, twice.

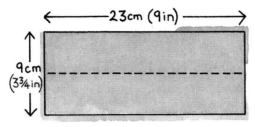

4 Tape one end to Joseph's 'chest' and then bind the folded tissue smoothly and evenly round the pipe cleaner to just below the end; turn and bind back again, taping the tissue at the top to hold it in place. Repeat for the other arm with the remaining half of the tissue. It will not look very neat, but do not worry - it does not have to as the arms will be hidden by his clothing.

5 Place two pipe cleaners together and push them into a turned paper ball, which is his head. Lower the pipe cleaners into the cone and tape them inside to hold.

Mary

6 To make the figure of Mary, fix two pipe cleaners into a ball as in step 5. Then draw a 14cm (5½in) semi-circle on white paper, with a 2cm (¾in) semi-circle at the centre. Mark a vertical line dividing the semi-circle in half, then cut it out.

7 Curve the paper round into a double-thickness cone, as step 2, and tape the join. Fit the two pipe cleaners protruding from the paper ball down into the cone and tape them inside so that the ends are level with the base of the cone. Bend the figure into a sitting position, the seat approximately 4cm (1½in) below the head and 3cm (1¼in) from the knees/top of cone.

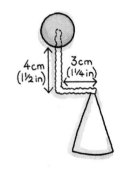

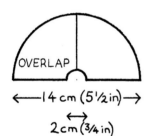

8 Fold a whole face tissue lengthways in half twice, then bind the body from the neck down to the knees, taping the ends to hold. Repeat with a second folded tissue, this time beginning at the knees and finishing at the neck.

9 Fit a pipe cleaner across the back of the figure, 1cm (³⁄₈in) below the head and extending equally at each side, to form arms. Tape to hold in place while binding securely with thread round the body. Then bind both arms as for Joseph, in steps 3 and 4.

Joseph's clothing

10 *The figures are now ready to dress. Use face tissues or table napkins as you wish, which will probably be dictated by the colours available. To make Joseph's robe, take a whole face tissue in the lighter brown, or a piece of*

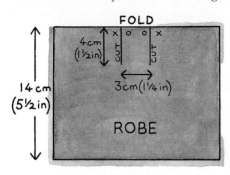

FOLD

4cm (1½in)

3cm (1¼in)

14cm (5½in)

ROBE

napkin, and fold over a section so that the tissue measures 14cm (5½in) deep. Make two 4cm (1½in) cuts equidistant from the centre and 3cm (1¼in) apart. Place this tissue over the front of the figure, with the central section of the fold under his chin. Fit the arms through the slits, then pin the corners marked X in the drawing over each other at the back of the neck. Catch the corners marked O over the shoulders with tape or a pin. Finally, draw the lower part of the tissue round the base of the cone and tape it at the back to hold it in position.

11 *For Joseph's beard, separate three strands of wool and then put them together again. Cut them in half, place the two pieces together, and repeat this twice more; then fold in half. Glue this to the lower half of the face, curving it round very slightly to form the top edge of his beard. Trim the cut ends to shape.*

12 *Joseph's darker brown cloak will need to be made from a table napkin. Cut a 28cm (11in) diameter semi-circle from a folded napkin. Drape it round the figure, taking the corners marked X on the drawing under the arms and round to the base of the cone at the centre back. Tape securely. Fold the arms round towards the front, inside the cloak.*

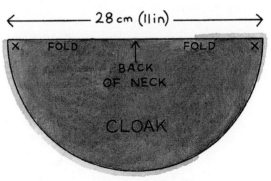

28cm (11in)

X   FOLD   FOLD   X

BACK OF NECK

CLOAK

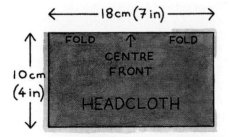

18cm (7in)

FOLD   FOLD

CENTRE FRONT

10cm (4in)

HEADCLOTH

13 *Cut another piece of folded tissue, 10cm x 18cm (4in x 7in), for Joseph's headcloth. Drape it over the head with the fold across the front. Fold in the corners at the back and surround the head tightly with a length of ribbon, crossing the ends at the back, with a pin to hold. Make a plaited braid (basics section 3), approximately 12 cm (4¾in) from the remaining ribbon and glue it round on top. Make another piece of braid about the same length in another shade. Fold it in half and glue it to the front of the robe, for his girdle.*

Holy family nativity

Mary's clothing

14 For Mary's hair, prepare four strands of wool as for Joseph's beard, (step 11) omitting the final fold. Brush well with wallpaper paste, ensuring it is thoroughly saturated, then apply to the head, framing the top and sides of the face; there is no need to cover the back of the head. Leave to dry. Drying can be hastened by removing the head and placing it in a very cool oven.

15 To make Mary's robe, follow the directions for Joseph's robe (step 10), using a napkin or tissue in the lighter blue.

16 Cut down a white tissue to measure 12cm (5in) deep, and fold it to 6cm (2½in). Drape the folded edge across the front of the head, gluing it at each side. For her mantle cut a folded semi-circle as for Joseph's cloak (step 12), using a darker blue napkin, but this time open it out into a circle and re-fold so that it measures 18cm (7in) from the fold to the bottom edge. Drape this over her head, taking the corners marked X on the drawing back under her arms and gluing them lightly to hold. Bring her arms round, under the mantle, and arrange the figure attractively. For her seat, build up the cotton reel by putting modelling clay etc on top of it to make it measure 5cm (2in) high. Glue her to this seat, under the mantle. Pin and glue as necessary to achieve the correct drape.

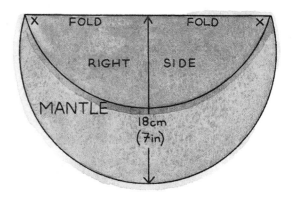

Baby Jesus

17 To make the baby Jesus, bend a pipe cleaner into three as shown here. Fit the small turned paper ball for the head on the protruding end. Fold a tissue lengthways into four and bind the body tightly, securing it with tape.

18 For the hair, cut a short piece off the single strand of honey coloured wool. Wind the remainder round a fingertip and slide it off. Slip the the short piece of wool you cut off through the centre and tie tightly. Cut the loops opposite the tie, then glue to the top of his head, with the cut ends overlapping his forehead. Fold a white tissue in half and wrap it round his head and body, gluing to hold. Trim the hair neatly.

Finishing of figures

19 Pin and glue the baby in its mother's arms, then draw features on all the figures, making short curved lines for the eyes, as shown here.

20 Cut a halo for each figure from white paper, using these patterns, and cover one side with gold ribbon. Cut the ribbon level with the paper, then cover the other side in the same way. Glue braid or pearls round the edge. Pin to the back of the head.

MARY AND JOSEPH

JESUS

HALOES

Stable

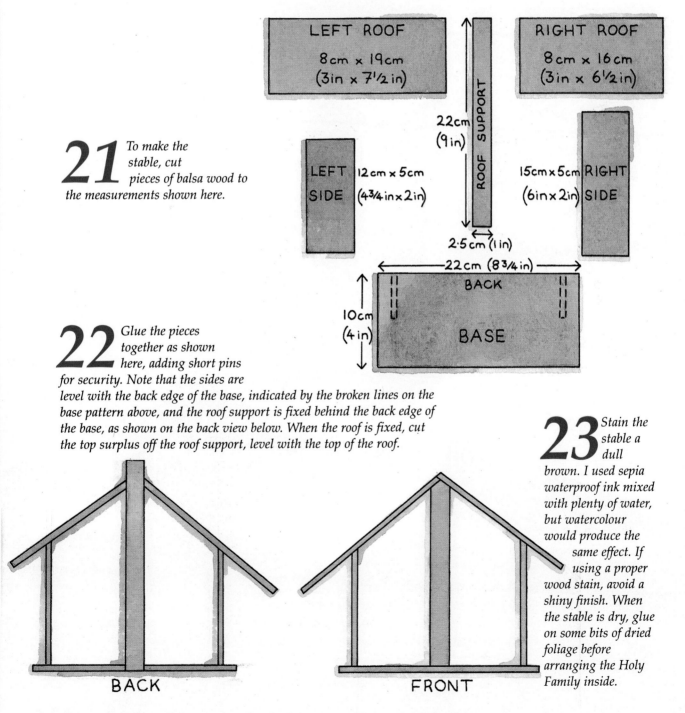

21 To make the stable, cut pieces of balsa wood to the measurements shown here.

LEFT ROOF
8cm x 19cm
(3in x 7½ in)

RIGHT ROOF
8cm x 16cm
(3in x 6½ in)

ROOF SUPPORT

22cm (9in)

LEFT SIDE 12cm x 5cm (4¾in x 2in)

15cm x 5cm (6in x 2in) RIGHT SIDE

2·5cm (1in)

22cm (8¾in)

BACK

10cm (4in)

BASE

22 Glue the pieces together as shown here, adding short pins for security. Note that the sides are level with the back edge of the base, indicated by the broken lines on the base pattern above, and the roof support is fixed behind the back edge of the base, as shown on the back view below. When the roof is fixed, cut the top surplus off the roof support, level with the top of the roof.

23 Stain the stable a dull brown. I used sepia waterproof ink mixed with plenty of water, but watercolour would produce the same effect. If using a proper wood stain, avoid a shiny finish. When the stable is dry, glue on some bits of dried foliage before arranging the Holy Family inside.

BACK

FRONT

Santa place cards

These rotund little characters, in traditional red or untraditionally in any bright colour you like, could play many roles at Christmas, even topping the cake. But here they are shown playing host to guests, showing them to their places at the table. Size one eggs were used and each figure is about 12cm (5in) high from his flat feet to the top of the pompon on the pointed hat.

1 First blow the egg and wash and dry it thoroughly (basics section 6).

2 The papier mâché covering protects and strengthens the shell as well as colouring it. Between a quarter and half a table napkin will be sufficient to cover the whole eggshell. Remove the embossed borders, then cut the remainder into pieces roughly 1-1.5cm ($^3/_8$–$^5/_8$in) square, separating the layers of tissue so that they are all single-ply. Make up a small amount of wallpaper paste and paste half the egg, using a thick brush. Begin covering the egg with a layer of tissue, overlapping the edges so that there are no gaps. Use the brush to pick up the tiny pieces of tissue, and brush more paste over once they are in position. Paste the rest of the egg and continue until there is a complete layer of tissue covering the shell, all the time brushing on more paste so that the tissue is saturated. Add several more layers of tissue in the same way, so that the egg is evenly covered.

MATERIALS

Size one egg.

Medium-weight white paper – for hat and pompon.

Thin card – for feet.

Pink face tissue – for the face.

Red or alternative colour two or three ply soft tissue table napkin etc – for the suit.

Matching felt – for the hat.

White felt – for the beard.

Black felt – for the feet.

20cm (8in) of white velvet tubing – for edging the hat.

White knitting yarn – for pompon; or use a 2cm (¾in) diameter purchased pompon.

Pink or red wooden bead, 7-8mm (¼in) in diameter – for his nose.

Scrap of black paper – for his eyes.

Very fine sandpaper.

Paper towel or rag.

Linseed oil, or alternative – for finishing (optional).

Modelling clay or plastic adhesive.

Wallpaper paste.

Clear adhesive.

3 Leave the egg in a warm place to dry, resting on a plastic bag, and turn it several times so that it dries evenly; on a windowsill in the sun is the best place. However, the paper covering needs to dry really hard, so it is a good idea to finish it off in the bottom of a cool oven. When doing this stand the egg point up on a baking tray, balanced on a curtain ring.

4 Trace this face shape on to a single layer of pink tissue, cut it out and paste it on to the egg, having the egg pointed end up and placing the pink tissue so that the centre of the bottom curve is level with the middle of the egg. Prepare some bits of pink tissue as before, and paste three or four layers over the pink area, overlapping the edge as necessary, but not too far. Allow to dry again.

FACE PATTERN

Santa place cards

5 This step is not essential but it does give a lovely smooth finish, and enhances the colour. First carefully sandpaper the egg all over, smoothing out any wrinkles. Then pour a tiny amount of oil on to a plate; I used linseed oil but olive oil or any good, clear cooking oil will be suitable. Wipe the paper towel or rag over the plate so that it picks up the oil evenly, then very, very gently smooth it over the egg so that just a little of the oil is absorbed, giving it a slight sheen and emphasising the colour. Take care, because it is easy to darken the colour too much; go carefully until you have just the depth of colour required.

6 Cut a 15cm (6in) diameter semi-circle of paper, cutting away a tiny semi-circle at the centre. Curve it round to form a cone that sits on the egg forming the foundation for his hat; remove it from the head and glue the join.

←——— 15 cm (6in) ———→

HAT
FOUNDATION

7 Cut this hat pattern in felt, then glue the felt smoothly round the hat cone, trimming the overlapping felt level with the lower edge. Glue it in position on the head.

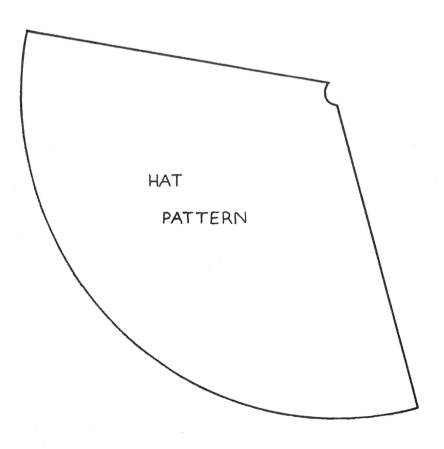

HAT

PATTERN

BEARD PATTERN

8 *Cut the beard in white felt using this pattern. Apply glue to the back as indicated by the wavy lines on the pattern, then stick it to the face, the top edges level with the lower edge of the hat. Glue velvet tubing round the bottom of the hat.*

9 *Glue the bead to the face for his nose, resting on his beard.*

10 *Cut the eyes in black paper and glue to the face as shown in the photograph. Either trace the eye pattern from here or cut it out freehand. Fold the black paper in half and cut it double to make two eyes; have the fold at the bottom and cut the upper curve first, finishing by cutting around the lower curve.*

EYE PATTERN

FOLD

11 *Cut the feet from thin card, using this pattern, and cover with black felt. Add a tiny wedge of modelling clay or alternative at the back (marked X on the pattern), then glue the feet under the egg, checking that the figure is correctly balanced and stands firmly.*

X
FEET PATTERN

12 *Trace this pompon pattern and cut it twice in paper. Make the pompon (basics section 4) and glue to the point of his hat.*

POMPON PATTERN

Christmas cottage

Children can enjoy this table centre. They can join in with the making, and then enjoy the finished cottage as a table centrepiece filled with small gifts or packets of sweets. The cottage itself measures 14cm x 18cm (5½in x 7in), plus the roof overhang all round, and is approximately 32cm (13in) to the top of its snow-capped chimney.

There is plenty of opportunity to adapt the design on the cottage if you wish; design your own windows and doors, arranging them as you please, and add your own finishing touches and decoration. The choice of colours can also be yours; various options are given in the instructions for colouring the doors, windows etc. I used a combination of white and coloured papers, adding texture with crayons. Details of the coloured writing paper I used are given in the suppliers section at the back of the book.

The instructions here explain how to make the cottage as shown in the photographs.

MATERIALS

50cm x 75cm (20in x 30in) sheet of artists' mounting board.

Cream coloured paper – for covering the walls.

White drawing (cartridge) paper – for windows etc.

Coloured paper – for the roof, doors, shutters, beams, chimney, step, hearts etc.

About 16cm x 20cm (6½in x 8in) of white card – for finishing the base.

30cm x 60cm (12in x 24in) of wadding or cotton wool – for the snow.

Crayons, felt pens, watercolour or poster paints etc – for colouring.

Black felt pens – fine for detail and medium for outlining.

Dark green two ply paper table napkin – for ivy and other greenery.

Metal hanger, small brass paper fasteners, bead, or alternatives – for door fittings.

Tiny bell, thick embroidery cotton, fine cord or thin string, hair grip – for front doorbell.

Thin card, tiny beads, and 6cm (2¼in) of curling ribbon (see suppliers section at back of book) – for wreath.

10cm (4in) of 2cm (¾in) wide ribbon, matching thread, and 10cm (4in) of 5mm (¼in) wide ribbon – for the back door bow.

Double-sided tape – for sticking roof wadding/cotton wool (optional).

Wallpaper paste – for greenery.

Glue stick – for sticking paper.

Clear adhesive – for other items.

Christmas cottage

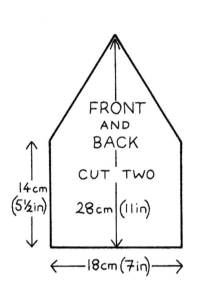

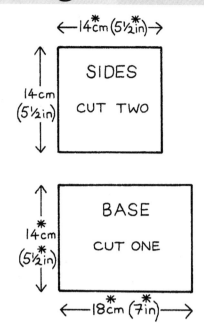

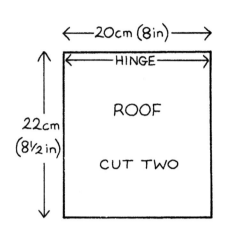

1 *Follow the measurements shown here to cut the pieces of mounting board for the front, back and roof. The measurements for the base and sides need to be adjusted to accommodate the thickness of the board. Mounting board is usually 1.5mm (¹/₁₆in) thick, but be sure to put two pieces of card together and measure the double thickness. If it is 3mm (¹/₈in), for example, this is the amount that must be deducted from the measurements for the base and sides that are shown with an asterisk in the drawings. If your measurement is different, adjust accordingly.*

2 *Tape the sides to the base, so that the edge of the base is against the inside of the side, as shown here. Tape the front and back to the base in the same way. Then bring all four walls up and tape them together where they meet. Lay the two roof pieces flat, with the two shorter edges flush together, and tape the join to form a hinge. Place the roof on top of the cottage and tape the join again, on top this time, at the angle it should be when in position.*

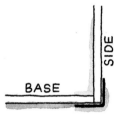

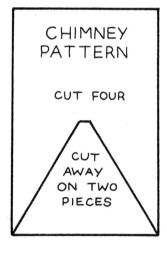

3 *Cut four pieces of mounting board for the chimney using this pattern: two of the full rectangle, and two with the inverted V-shape cut away. Join the pieces together to make the chimney shape, taping the V-shaped pieces between the plain ones.*

4 *Cut a 9cm x 18cm (3¹/₂in x 7in) piece of coloured paper and stick it round the chimney, trimming it level with the card round the lower edge. Cut down each corner of the paper above the chimney, fold the paper down, and stick it neatly inside the chimney. On the outside of the chimney rule lines with a felt pen to divide the surface into 'bricks'.*

5 *Cut pieces of cream paper to cover the walls, as follows.*

Front and back – two pieces each:

10cm x 14cm (4in x 5¹/₂in) – for the top section.

8cm x 18cm (3¹/₄in x 7in) – for the centre section.

12cm x 18cm (4³/₄in x 7in) – for the lower section.

Sides – two pieces each:

4.5cm x 14cm (1¹/₂in x 5¹/₂in) – for the upper section.

12cm x 14cm (4³/₄in x 5¹/₂in) – for the lower section.

6 Rule lines on each wall to indicate the two horizontal beams, in the positions shown below. Glue the sections of cream paper into place, level with the marked lines, so that the joins will be hidden under the beams. Fold the excess paper on the top section inside the cottage, and stick it down. Stick the excess at the bottom underneath the base.

7 Prepare the beams by ruling lines on either brown or white paper, following the measurements here. Draw the beams 5mm (¼in) apart, and do not cut them out.

For each of the front and back:
One 1cm x 15cm (³⁄₈in x 6in) - upper horizontal beam.
One 1cm x 18cm (³⁄₈in x 7in) - lower horizontal beam.
Two 1cm x 20cm (³⁄₈in x 8in) - diagonal roof beams.
Two 7mm x 6cm (¼in x 2³⁄₈in) - upper vertical beams.

For each side:
One 1cm x 14cm (³⁄₈in x 5½in) - horizontal beam.

For each corner:
One 2cm x 14cm (³⁄₄in x 5½in) - vertical support beam.

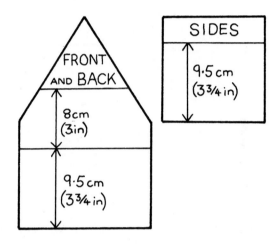

8 If you are using white paper you will need to colour the beams using either crayons, felt pens or paints. Although I used brown paper, which did not need colouring, I rubbed a sepia coloured pencil all over the surface, which gave it a lovely textured effect, resembling very old weathered wood. When the beams are coloured, outline them freehand with a black felt pen, then cut them out with scissors, not a knife, so that the lines will be a little uneven and will look more natural. Score the corner beams lengthways down the centre. Shown here are the effects of different techniques used on coloured and white paper.

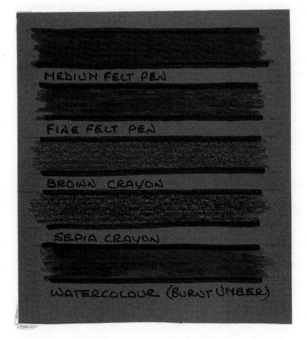

Christmas cottage

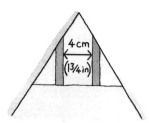

9 Glue the horizontal beam to each side wall, over the join in the cream paper. Glue the two upper vertical beams to the front and back 4cm (1¾in) apart, with the lower edge resting on the join in the cream paper, as shown here. Then glue the two horizontal beams in place, over the joins. Glue the vertical support beams into position, folding them round the corners. Finally, glue the diagonal roof beams level with the top edges of the front and back, trimming them to shape at each end to butt neatly where they join.

Double windows with shutters feature on the front and back of the cottage.

10 Trace the windows on to white paper, adapting the pattern here if you wish, to make up the windows you require. For the cottage as shown prepare the following:

Three double windows with shutters.
Two triple windows without shutters.
One double window without shutters.
Three single windows without shutters.

Colour the window panes dark blue, the frames light brown, and the shutters green, using crayons, felt pens or watercolours. Then go over the lines that are shown on the pattern in black, using a fine felt tip for the panes and the detail on the shutters, and a thicker felt pen for outlining. Cut them all out, cutting away the diamond shapes on the shutters with a sharp knife.

WINDOWS PATTERN

11 Trace the door frame plus the step on to brown or white paper, but do not cut it out yet. Prepare the frame in the same way as the beams. Then cut out round the inside of the frame only. Cut a 10cm x 8cm (4in x 3in) piece of coloured or white paper for the door (adding colour and texture as you wish) and glue it behind the door frame. Then cut round the outer edge of the frame. Rule lines on the door as shown in the drawing. Trace the step again, in grey; outline it and cut it out. Glue it into position below the door frame. Prepare the back door in exactly the same way, but follow the broken line on the drawing for the outer edge of the frame, and move the tracing down so the bottom of the door meets the step, before tracing the step.

A festive wreath hangs on the front door.

The back door is decorated with a large butterfly bow.

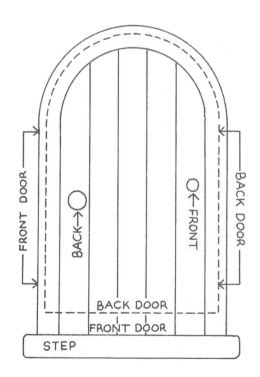

Christmas cottage

12 *Cut two pieces of coloured paper 25cm x 25cm (10in x 10in) and cover the underside of the roof, gluing each piece level with the hinged top inside, with the paper then overhanging the outside edges of the roof by 2cm (1in). Cut across the corners of the overhang, as shown here, fold the surplus neatly over and glue it to the top of the roof.*

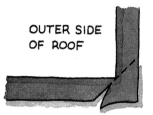

OUTER SIDE OF ROOF

13 *Place the doors and windows on the walls to decide their arrangement in relation to each other, then measure and mark the position accurately before sticking them neatly into position.*

14 *Trace the tiny hearts given here on to pink paper, cut them out and stick them to the walls above the windows as shown in the photograph.*

15 *For the snow on the roof, cut a piece of wadding or cotton wool a little larger than the entire roof. Place it over the roof to make sure the coloured paper is not visible through it. If it is, cover the top of the roof with white paper or thin card. To attach the wadding or cotton wool, stick strips of double-sided tape all round the edge of the roof and across the centre top join. Alternatively use clear adhesive, but take care to use the minimum necessary, and spread it thoroughly.*

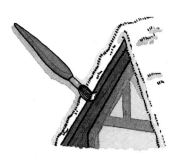

16 *Place the wadding over the roof, overhanging the edge of the roof all round, and press it against the tape. Then trim off the excess, about 3mm (1/8in) from the edge of the roof. Run a trail of glue along the cut edges of the roof and smooth the edge of the wadding down over the edge.*

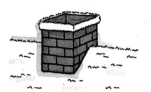

17 *Fit the chimney on top in the centre. Mark the position with pins, then remove the chimney and cut away the wadding underneath. Glue the chimney to the roof, pushing the cut edges of the wadding up against it. Cut a very narrow strip of wadding or cotton wool and glue it round the top edge of the chimney.*

18 To make the ivy-clad walls, remove the embossed borders from the napkin and cut the remainder into 2-3cm (1in) wide strips. Separate the plies. Place a strip on a flat surface - a dinner plate is good - and brush it generously with wallpaper paste. Lift one end with something like a fine skewer, thin knitting needle or small pointed scissors. If, when you attempt to lift the soggy tissue, it disintegrates - it is exactly right! Scrape up the crumpled bits of torn tissue, then press, poke and prod them into place on the cottage, beginning with the base of each creeper at the sides of the cottage, so that they cover the side walls and then climb round to the front and back, as shown here. Push the small bits of tissue into clusters of 'leaves', allowing them to creep in all directions. When the walls are covered to your satisfaction, leave to dry thoroughly.

19 Use paper fasteners or beads for door-knobs, and a picture hanger for the door knocker.

20 Make a hole in the beam above the front door, close to the vertical corner support, and push a hairgrip through from the outside. Fix the bell through the loop of the hairgrip with a short length of thick cotton or fine cord or string, making a loop at the bottom. Pinch the ends of the hairgrip together.

21 The wreath on the front door is made like the ivy. Trace the pattern given here on to thin card and cut it out. Cover one side with pasted tissue, pushing it tightly together to build it up. When quite dry, glue on tiny beads and make a 2cm ($^3/_4$in) wide bow by folding back the cut ends of a 6cm ($2^1/_4$in) length of 9mm ($^3/_8$in) wide ribbon so that they overlap at the back. Bind the centre tightly with matching thread and glue in place. Fold a 15cm (6in) length of curling ribbon in half and cut each half into very narrow strips. Curl (basics section 7), then fix the fold behind the bottom of the wreath with tape.

WREATH PATTERN

22 The back door is decorated with a giant butterfly bow made from 10cm (4in) of fancy 2cm ($^3/_4$in) wide ribbon (basics section 2, but note the wider ribbon), with a 10cm (4in) length of 5mm ($^1/_4$in) wide green ribbon folded in half to form streamers behind. Fix the wreath and bow with tape or glue.

23 For snow around the cottage, cut narrow — about 5mm ($^1/_4$in) — strips of wadding or cotton wool and glue the cut edge along the base of each wall, applying the glue to the wall. Cut a piece of thin white card a little larger than the base. Round off the corners and glue it underneath, to protect the snow.

24 Trace the animals' bowls as given here on to coloured paper, outline and letter, then cut out and glue either side of the back door.

Angel maypole

Just for a change, forget the traditional snow and sleigh and
jingle bells. Instead, decorate your table with this centrepiece
of angels in lacy pinafores dancing round a tinsel maypole.
The angels are approximately 18cm (7in) tall, with a wing
span of 10cm (4in). The maypole should be between 25 and
30cm (10 and 12in) high.

Angels

1 *For a figure, draw a 28cm (11in) diameter semi-circle on white paper, using compasses, with a 2cm (³⁄₄in) semi-circle at the centre. Measure point B at the end of a straight line 6cm (2³⁄₈in) from A and rule a line between B and C. Measure and mark the centrepoint between B and D, then rule the line C-E straight through it. Cut out, cutting away the shaded area.*

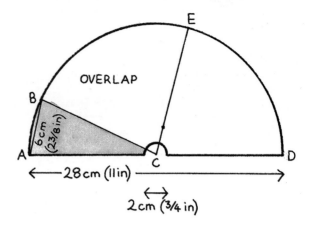

OVERLAP

6cm (2³⁄₈in)

28cm (11in)

2cm (³⁄₄in)

MATERIALS

For the six angels and maypole:

Medium-weight white paper – for body foundations.

Coloured paper (tissue, crêpe, gift-wrap etc) – for dresses.

Two paper doilies about 20cm (8in) in diameter – for pinafores.

Thin white card – for wings.

Six flesh tinted turned paper balls, 3.5cm (1³⁄₈in) in diameter – for heads.

Six pipe cleaners or craft stems, 15cm (6in) long – for fixing the heads.

2.7m (3yd) of 1cm (³⁄₈in) wide lace – for collars.

Twilleys stranded embroidery wool, or knitting yarn – for hair.

45cm (½yd) of tiny pearl bead trimming – for hair circlet.

White glitter powder and white PVA adhesive – for the wings.

Silvery-grey curling ribbon – for joining angels to maypole.

Sepia watercolour pencil, ballpoint pen etc – for features.

Strip of tinsel – length required depends on density of tinsel and the height of the maypole.

25-30cm (10-12in) of wooden dowelling 5-10mm (¼in–³⁄₈in) in diameter – for the maypole.

Candle base and modelling clay or Stick 'n' Fix – to hold the maypole.

Pins – for fixing the wings.

Adhesive tape.

Glue stick – for sticking paper.

Clear adhesive – for sticking other items.

---

2 *Curve one half of the paper round over the other, so that the two straight edges are level with the ruled line, making a cone of double thickness paper. Tape the whole join outside, and at intervals inside.*

3 *Make a template for the dress pattern (see basics section 8) by cutting out a quarter circle of stiff paper to the measurements shown. If you are using a thin paper, like tissue or crêpe, make the radius about 17cm (6³⁄₄in),*

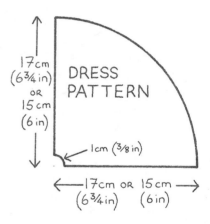

17cm (6³⁄₄in) OR 15cm (6in)

DRESS PATTERN

1cm (³⁄₈in)

17cm OR 15cm (6³⁄₄in) (6in)

but if the paper is thicker use a radius of only about 15cm (6in). Cut away 1cm (³⁄₈in) at the corner.

4 *Cut the dress in coloured paper and wrap it smoothly round the figure, gluing the overlap at the back to join. If you are using thin paper tuck it neatly up inside the cone, but if you are using thicker paper trim it level with the lower edge.*

23

Angel maypole

5 Cut a 3cm (1¼in) circle out of the centre of each doily, then cut each into three equal sections.

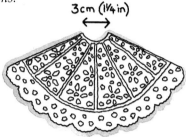

3cm (1¼in)

6 Mark the centre front of the cone 3cm (1¼in) from the top, then position the centre top of the doily at this point and wrap the sides round the cone so that the lower corners overlap at the back. Glue or tape these corners to hold the doily in place.

3 cm (1¼in)

7 Bend a pipe cleaner in half and push the bent end into a turned paper ball. Then lower the cut ends down into the cone and tape them inside; use tweezers to insert the tape, then press it down.

8 Cut three 15cm (6in) lengths of lace. Gather the straight edge of one piece and draw it up tightly round the neck, securing the cut ends at the back. Repeat with the other two pieces, drawing each up tightly close under the previous one.

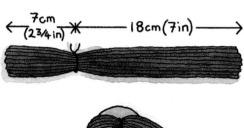

7cm (2¾in)   18cm (7in)

9 Separate twelve 76cm (30in) strands of wool; if using knitting yarn, you may need fewer. Then put nine together again and fold them into three. Tie this skein loosely with a single strand, 7cm (2¾in) from one end. Glue the tied area across the top of the head, then take the shorter end smoothly down one side of the face and round to the back, gluing it into place all the way. Now take the longer piece over the other side of the face and round to the back, but having crossed over the shorter end, take the skein up and continue going round and round, to cover the whole head, ending on the crown.

10 Fold the remaining three strands in half three times, then tie in a loose knot and catch the ends underneath, to form a bun. Stitch or glue this over the crown. Circle the base of the bun with a 7.5cm (3in) length of pearl beads. Stitch the join at the back to avoid getting glue on the hair.

11 For the features, mark round dots for the eyes, and for the nose mark a short fine line between and level with the lower edge of the eyes (basics section 5).

12 Transfer the wings pattern to folded stiff paper (basics section 8) to make a template. Open this out to cut the wings in white card. Place the open wings on a sheet of clean paper and score the centre line. Spread liberally with PVA adhesive, then sprinkle glitter powder thickly over it, shaking off the excess. When thoroughly dry, fix the wings to the back of the figure with a pin near each end of the fold.

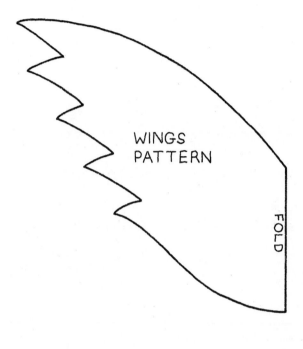

WINGS PATTERN

FOLD

13 Make five more figures in the same way.

Maypole

14 Tie one end of the tinsel tightly to the top of the dowelling with curling ribbon. Wind the tinsel round and round the dowelling until the dowelling is completely covered. Tie securely at the bottom. Fix the base in a candle holder with modelling clay or Stick 'n' Fix.

15 Cut six 75cm (30in) lengths of curling ribbon. Make a tiny circular loop at one end of each piece by winding it round your fingertip and gluing or taping the overlap to join. Thread a 15cm (6in) length of ribbon through all six loops, then tie the ribbon round the maypole, just below the top, distributing the loops evenly around the maypole. Trim off the surplus ribbon close to the knot. Circle the top of the maypole with a short length of tinsel to give it a neat finish.

16 With the maypole in the centre of the table, arrange the angels round it. Then twist the six loose ends of curling ribbon a few times before fixing them to the back of the wings by removing the top pin and pushing it through the ribbon before replacing it. Either trim off or curl the remaining ribbon.

Candle wreaths

A pretty base is the ideal setting for any candle, and a ready-made polystyrene ring is often an easy and effective starting point. Two basic designs are shown here, each in two colourways: four 20cm (8in) tapered candles are set into a 22cm (9in) diameter polystyrene ring, and the 10cm (4in) single fat candle stands in the centre of a 12cm (5in) ring.

In each case I have surrounded the wreath with butterfly bows. On the large wreaths the red tartan plaid exactly matches the candles, giving a vibrant Christmas look, while the green tartan contrasts with the cream candles, making a more elegant effect.

On the small wreaths the bows are made from a dark green sheer ribbon with satin stripes, which matches the candle, but in each case the bow is made with double ribbon and has another shade inside. The ribbon roses tone with this ribbon.

Large wreaths

MATERIALS

Polystyrene ring 22cm (9in) in diameter.	12 small gold-painted pine cones – for red candles.
Four tapered candles 20cm (8in) high.	60cm (³/₄yd) tiny seed pearl trimming – for cream candles.
6m (7yd) of 39mm (1¹/₂in) wide red tartan plaid ribbon – for red candles.	Matching or black sewing thread.
2.5m (3yd) of 39mm (1¹/₂in) wide green tartan plaid ribbon – for cream candles.	Eight short florists' stub wires to fix the cones – wreath with red candles.
4m (4¹/₂yd) of 39mm (1¹/₂in) wide forest green 'Sheer Majesty' gold-edged sheer organza ribbon – for cream candles.	Pins.
	Clear adhesive.

1 For either of the large wreaths, make four holes equally round the ring to hold the candles. To do this make a hole slightly smaller than the candle and remove the bits of polystyrene; then force the candle in and press it down. Remove the candles again.

Candle wreaths

2 *Bind the wreath tightly with ribbon, beginning by anchoring it firmly to the ring with two or three pins. In the case of the red ribbon just overlap the edges of the ribbon, but for the gold-edged organza overlap half the width of the ribbon so that the gold stripe underneath shows through the layer on top. Pin securely again when the whole ring is covered. Carefully cut away just enough ribbon over the holes to allow the candles to be replaced, pinning any cut edges to prevent them pulling away.*

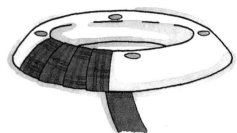

3 *To make the butterfly bows, cut a 30cm (12in) length of ribbon. Mark the centre A and points B and C, shown here, against the top edge, 7cm (2¾in) from each end.*

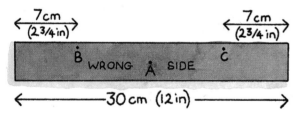

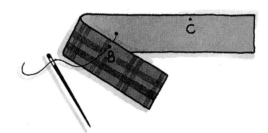

4 *Thread a needle with matching or black thread and bring it forward through point A from the back. Curve the left hand end of the ribbon round and bring the needle forward through point B.*

5 *Curve the right hand end round and repeat for point C.*

6 *Draw up and gather up through point D.*

7 Take the needle down behind and bring it forward through point E.

8 Now take the needle up, over the top and down the back, bringing it forward again through point F.

9 Finally, gently draw the whole thing up, arranging the bow as you do so, and bind the thread tightly round the centre several times, finishing securely at the back. Cut an inverted V-shape at each end of the ribbon.

10 Make eight bows. Pin one below each candle, then pin the others evenly in between. Use two pins for each bow, either side of the centre, pushing them between the gathers so that they cannot be seen.

11 For the red candles wreath, fix stub wires round the base of eight cones, twisting the wires to hold, then push them into the side of the ring between the bows. Glue the remaining four cones on top of the ring, between the candles.

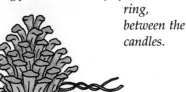

12 For the cream candles, make eight circles of pearls just large enough to slip over the candles and fit round the base. To do this, cut the pearls the correct length, then put a tiny blob of adhesive at each end and allow it to become tacky. When it is almost dry, push the two ends together. Leave until thoroughly dry, then slip two rings over each candle. Glue a pair of pearls in the middle of each bow.

Candle wreaths

Small wreaths

1 *For either of the smaller wreaths, pin holly, ivy or other greenery over the ring to mask the polystyrene.*

2 *Pin the circle of card underneath the base.*

3 *To make a bow, cut a 30cm (12in) length of dark green ribbon and place it flat. Pin a similar piece of chartreuse or violet ribbon on top. Make the bow as described for the large wreaths. Make six bows altogether.*

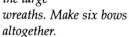

4 *To make the golden roses, cut a 50cm (½yd) length of Dijon ribbon and make ribbon roses as in basics section 1, but fold the ribbon in half as you work, beginning with the fold at the bottom, as shown here. Make six roses.*

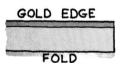

GOLD EDGE

FOLD

5 *To make the violet (grape) roses, follow the directions for making ribbon roses (basics section 1) but cut a 30cm (12in) length of ribbon so as to make extra petals. Make six roses.*

6 *Stitch a rose in the centre of each bow, then pin the bows evenly round the ring. Use two pins for each bow, either side of the centre, pushing them between the gathers so that they cannot be seen.*

Carolling choristers

These choirboys are quick and easy to make, and at 12cm (4¾in) high offer plenty of potential. For instance, this cheerful little group of three, standing on the windowsill in a porch or hall, would provide the perfect seasonal greeting to welcome Christmas visitors. Arrange a set of four on the dinner table, or around the Christmas pudding or cake. Stand them under tall candles on a mantlepiece, or leave out the inner filling and hang them from the Christmas tree.

Carolling choristers

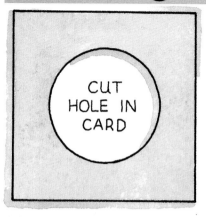

CUT HOLE IN CARD

1 Cut a 3cm (1¼in) diameter hole in the centre of the card.

2 Cut a strip of white paper 8cm (3in) deep and about 30cm (12in) long. Roll it up, then push it into the hole and allow it to open out to fit the sides snugly, making sure the cut edges are level. Tape the join and remove from the card. Roll up strips of 8cm (3in) deep waste paper and push them, one at a time, into the tube, encouraging them to open out inside. Continue until the tube is firmly filled; this will give it solidity and weight.

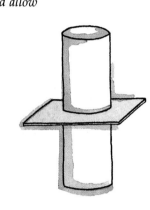

MATERIALS

Medium-weight white paper – for body and music sheet.

Red paper-backed foil gift-wrap, or alternative paper – for cassock.

5cm (2in) square of thin card – for body template.

Waste paper – for stuffing the body.

Flesh-tinted turned paper ball, 3.5cm (1⅜in) in diameter – for the head.

Pipe cleaner.

50cm (½yd) of 1.5cm (⅝in) deep white lace – for collar.

5cm (2in) of 1.5mm (1⁄16in) wide black satin ribbon – for bow.

Nine 76cm (30in) strands of Twilleys stranded embroidery wool, or fine knitting yarn.

Black ink or fine ballpoint pen – for music.

Sepia watercolour pencil, or ballpoint pen – for features.

Adhesive tape.

Double-sided tape.

Glue stick (optional).

Adhesive.

3 Cut an 8cm x 12cm (3in x 5in) strip of red paper. Wrap it round the tube and glue the join. Trace the sleeve pattern given here on to folded white paper and cut out. Cover with red paper. Run a trail of glue inside each sleeve as indicated by the wavy line, and press together.

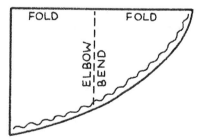

FOLD   FOLD

ELBOW BEND

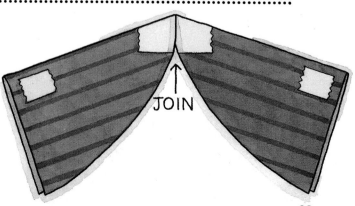

JOIN

4 Place the top edges of the two sleeves together and join with tape. Turn over, so that the tape is on the inside, and fold each arm lightly in half, as indicated by the broken line on the pattern, to resemble bent elbows. Then fix the centrepoint to the back of the figure, over the join and just below the top edge, using double-sided tape. Add two more small bits of tape near the edge of each sleeve, as shown, and use these to fix the sleeves in position, as in the photograph.

5 Examine the turned paper ball to choose the best surface for the face, indicating it with an arrow on top of the head. Bend the pipe cleaner in half and push the two ends into the ball.

6 To make the collar, join the cut ends of the lace to form a circle. Gather the top edge, draw up tightly and secure, leaving a 1.5-2cm (½-¾in) hole in the centre. Then lower the pipe cleaner through the lace and into the body.

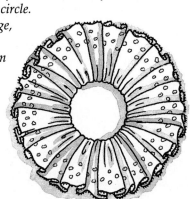

7 For the hair, separate the strands of embroidery wool and then place them together again. If using knitting yarn, you may need less. Cut in half three times, to measure 9.5cm (3¾in), and tie the centre tightly with a single strand. Glue the tied area to the crown of the head, spreading the strands out smoothly and evenly all round, and gluing the head to hold the wool in place. Cut to shape, following the photograph for guidance, then remove the head to make it easier to trim the hair neatly and tidily, layering the top hair at the back so that it clears the collar and lies flat on the head. Replace the head and collar on top of the body tube, this time gluing them permanently.

8 Make a tiny butterfly bow (basics section 2) from the ribbon and glue it under his chin.

9 Draw the eyes, nose and mouth. (See basics section 5).

10 Trace the sheet of music on to white paper (basics section 8). Draw lines and music on it, as indicated. Cut out, then score and fold as indicated by the broken line on the pattern. Stroke the pages to curl them slightly (basics section 7). Glue the bottom edge of the sheet music to the figure, resting on the front corners of the sleeves.

1. Ribbon roses

Ideally use a single-face satin ribbon for roses, except for the 3mm (1/8in) ribbon, which comes only in double-face satin. This 3mm ribbon makes a miniature rose and it is sensible to become familiar with the technique before attempting it, as it is a little fiddly.

Choose a suitable colour; the Offray range of ribbons used on the projects in this book offers a wide choice of realistic shades that are as close as you can get to nature. On the other hand, unnatural colours can look just as attractive in certain situations. Sable brown roses on a cream background, for instance, can look stunning, as can mauve or blue.

Width of ribbon 3mm (1/8in)
Length required 11cm (4 1/2in)

Width of ribbon 7mm (1/4in)
Length required 15cm (6in)

Width of ribbon 9mm (3/8in)
Length required 20cm (8in)

Width of ribbon 15mm (5/8in)
Length required 30-40cm (12-16in)

Rose made with 3m (3yd) of 39mm (1 1/2in) wide sheer organza ribbon, folded in half, as used on a small wreath in this book

1 *Cut off the required amount of ribbon; this will depend on the number of petals wanted but the amounts shown above are a good average.*

2 *Fold the corner over, as shown by the broken line, bringing point A down to meet point B.*

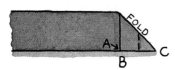

3 *Bring point C over to meet points A and B.*

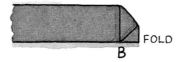

4 *Roll the ribbon around three or four times, with the folded corner inside, to form a tight tube, and make a few holding stitches through the base.*

6 *When the tube again lies parallel with the remaining ribbon, take a couple of stitches through the base to hold the petal you have just made.*

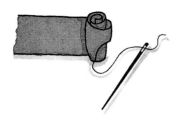

5 *To make the petal, fold the ribbon down so that the edge is aligned with the tube. Then curve the ribbon around the tube to form a cone, keeping the top of the tube level with the diagonal fold.*

7 *Continue to make petals with the remainder of the ribbon, sewing each one to the base of the flower before starting the next.*

8 *Shape the rose as you work by gradually making the petals a little more open. Finish with the cut end tucked neatly underneath the base of the completed rose.*

2. Butterfly bows

Use single-face or double-face satin ribbon. All the measurements for these bows are variable, so the length required will depend on the ribbon width, the effect you wish to create, and the length you want the streamers to be.

Experience and experimentation will determine your own personal preferences, but the examples shown at the foot of the page are a good average to work on for a standard shaped bow made from the narrower ribbon widths.

With a very wide ribbon the directions differ slightly – see the instructions for the candle wreaths elsewhere in the book.

1 *On the wrong (dull) side of the ribbon,* mark point A at the centre, close to the lower edge as shown here. Mark points B and C equally either side of the centre, close to the top edge. Cut the ends in an inverted V-shape, or do this afterwards if you prefer - and don't do it at all for the narrowest ribbons.

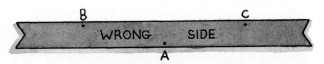

2 *Hold the ribbon with the wrong side facing you. Using matching thread, bring the needle through point A from the back. Then curve* the left end round and bring the needle through point B; curve the right end round and bring the needle through point C. Draw up the thread so that B and C are on top of A.

3 *Take the needle up and through the centre top of the back length of the ribbon - marked D on the drawing. Then take it down at the back and bring it through to the front again to emerge at point E on the drawing.*

4 *Take the thread up and over the top and wrap it tightly round the middle several times, drawing up and shaping the bow as you do so. Finish off neatly and securely at the back.*

| Width of ribbon 1.5mm (¹/₁₆in) Length required 6cm (2¹/₂in) | Width of ribbon 3mm (¹/₈in) Length required 8cm (3¹/₄in) | Width of ribbon 7mm (¹/₄in) Length required 10cm (4in) | Width of ribbon 9mm (³/₈in) Length required 12.5cm (5in) | Width of ribbon 15mm (⁵/₈in) Length required 15cm (6in) |

3. Plaited braid

Each braid in one colour

Each braid in two colours

Multicoloured braid with three colours

Use 1.5mm (¹/₁₆in) wide satin ribbon. To estimate the amount you will need, measure the length of braid that you require, add a third of that length, and then multiply the result by three. For example, for a 15cm (6in) length of braid you will require:

15cm + 5cm (6in + 2in) = 20cm (8in)
x 3 = 60cm (24in)

If you want to make a multicoloured braid, calculate the amount of each colour separately, ie not multiplying by three. In the above example this would mean 20cm of each of three colours.

1 When using ribbon of one colour, fold the ribbon into three, but cut only one fold. Glue one end of the shorter piece inside the fold of the longer piece, as shown here, and pinch together. Glue in the same way if using two colours. If making a multicoloured braid, just glue all three cut ends together.

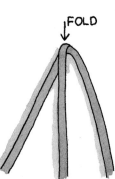

FOLD

2 Push a pin through the glued end and secure it to a drawing board or something similar. Then begin to plait very evenly, making sure that the strands of ribbon are always flat; never fold them over. Keep the ribbon taut, and draw the plait very firmly between the fingertips every 2-3cm (an inch or so) to make it smooth and even. Hold the ends together with a paper clip.

3 Glue the braid into place, spreading the glue on the braid just beyond the point where you intend to cut it, to ensure that it does not unravel. Press the cut ends down well, adding a little more glue if necessary.

4. Making a pompon

The most common mistake when making a pompon is to stop winding the yarn round the foundation circles before the central hole is absolutely full. The result is a sadly wilting specimen. But if the central hole is so full that the needle cannot be pushed through any more, the finished pompon will be round and firm.

I usually work with double yarn, but when making large pompons I speed things up by working with four strands at a time. Use sharp scissors to shape the pompon, clipping it down to a good, firm, rounded ball.

1 *To make the pattern for the pompon draw a circle slightly smaller than the required diameter of the finished pompon. Draw an inner circle in the centre in roughly the same proportion to the outer ring as the one shown here.*

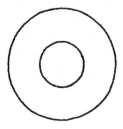

2 *Cut the pattern twice in medium-weight paper for a small pompon, stiff paper for a slightly bigger one, and thin card for a large one. Cut out the inner circle and place the two rings together.*

3 *Thread a tapestry needle with a long length of yarn, and work with it double. Wrap it closely and evenly round and round the two rings.*

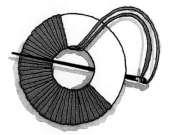

4 *Add more yarn as necessary, until the central hole is so full that the needle will not go through any more.*

5 *Push pointed scissors through the yarn, between the paper circles, and cut the yarn all round, keeping the scissors between the paper.*

4. Making a pompon continued

6 Slip a length of yarn (or use fine crochet cotton for greater strength) between the circles to surround the yarn in the centre.

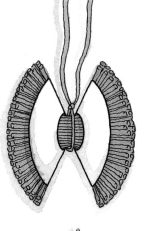

7 Knot together, pulling tight, then cut and pull away the paper.

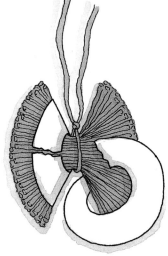

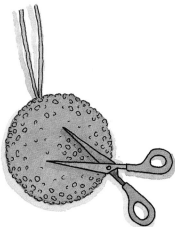

8 Holding the ties in one hand, trim the pompon severely with sharp scissors, to make a neat, firm, round ball.

5. Drawing faces and features

My own preference is to draw the features with a sepia watercolour pencil, or an ordinary sepia crayon, because it gives a softer effect than black. But use a black ballpoint pen for stronger definition, if you prefer. Avoid ink or felt tip pens etc on turned paper balls as anything wet may run and be absorbed by the soft paper.

The examples shown here demonstrate how a couple of dots and a few simple lines can create a character.

1 The little boy (right) has a tiny nose level with the bottom of the eyes, and a broad grin. I draw the features first with a soft lead pencil, so that I can keep rubbing them out with a soft eraser until I get the expression just as I want it. Then I colour in the eyes with a dry sepia pencil, and the outline of the eyes and mouth is drawn in with the pencil slightly moistened.

2 The little girl (centre) has wide eyes and a demure smile, with just a hint of eyebrows.

3 The grey-haired granny (left) has more definite eyebrows and the small curved lines make softer eyes for an older person. The principle for them all is the same – keep it simple.

6. Blowing an egg

When emptied of their contents ordinary hen's eggs are so light they are ideal for hanging from the tree as decorations. Pasting the outside with a covering of papier mâché, as for the baubles in this book, gives the delicate shell strength or resilience. Make sure that you clean out the egg thoroughly before you start, and that no remnants of egg yolk remain inside, to avoid any unpleasant smells later!

1 Make small holes at each end of the egg with a darning needle, the hole at the rounded end of the egg slightly larger than the other; begin by gently scratching the surface before finally breaking through the shell, and then enlarge the hole to the required size with the point of the needle.

3 Holding the egg over a basin, blow through the hole at the pointed end until the shell is empty.

BLOW

2 Push the needle inside and gently stir it around to break up the yolk and mix it with the white.

4 Wash the eggshell very thoroughly in detergent, inside and out. Then set it, pointed end up, in an egg-cup until thoroughly dry; a cool oven hurries things along, and ensures no moisture remains inside.

7. Stroking and curling paper

Stroking paper to curl it is easy and yet so effective in many different situations. The most obvious one is for crêpe paper flowers, when it makes the most wonderfully realistic petals and leaves. But it can give all kinds of items another dimension.

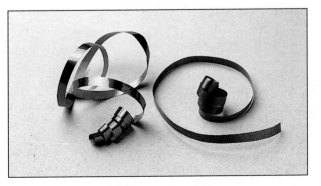

On the gift-wrap counter you will also find a special curling ribbon in a range of vivid colours including silver and gold. This is curled in seconds; the more you stroke it, the more it curls.

7. Stroking and curling paper continued

1 *All you need for curling is a blunt knife and your thumb. I use a small kitchen vegetable knife because I find the size and shape easy, but it is simply a matter of what you have available and what suits you best. Holding the paper or ribbon in one hand, and the knife in the other, draw the part to be curled firmly between the blade (on top) and your thumb (underneath), flicking off at the end.*

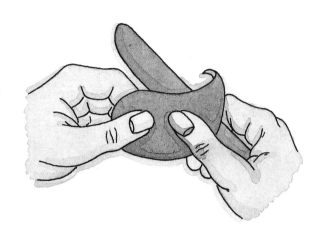

2 *Repeat two or three times until you have achieved the amount of curl required.*

8. Transferring a tracing and making a template

When you need to reproduce the outline of a pattern from the book on to a surface you cannot see through, such as thick paper or card, trace if off and transfer it as described here.

1 *Trace the outline of the pattern from the book on to household greaseproof paper.*

2 *Turn the paper over and rub over the back of the outline with a soft pencil.*

3 *Turn the paper back to the front again and fix it securely to the surface to which the tracing is to be transferred. Then draw over the outline again with a firm point, such as a ballpoint pen, hard pencil or knitting needle.*

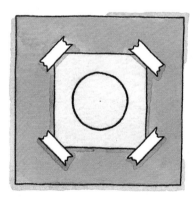

4 *When the tracing paper is removed, a clear outline should remain. If necessary, clean up the paper around it with an eraser.*

5 *To make a template transfer the tracing of the outline as described above on to stiff paper, or thin card if extra rigidity is required. Cut it out and use this as a pattern round which to cut your crêpe paper, fabric etc.*